Jean,

You are unique!

I am forever grateful,

John Bell
Winter Retreat
2015

S.N.O.W. Everyday!

Self-Awareness and New Opportunities in Worship

Six Weeks of Discovering Your Uniqueness While in God's Presence

Dr. Patricia E. Coker-Bell

Copyright © 2010 by Dr. Patricia E. Coker-Bell

S.N.O.W. Everyday!
by Dr. Patricia E. Coker-Bell

Printed in the United States of America

ISBN 9781609570859

All rights reserved solely by the author. The author guarantees all contents are original and do not infringe upon the legal rights of any other person or work. No part of this book may be reproduced in any form without the permission of the author. The views expressed in this book are not necessarily those of the publisher.

Unless otherwise indicated, Bible quotations are taken from Holy Bible, New International Version of the Bible. Copyright © 1973, 1978, 1984 by International Bible Society.

www.xulonpress.com

This journal is dedicated to my paternal grandmother,
Luvenue Carpenter, my maternal grandmother,
Lucy Garris, and my mother, Blanche Garris Coker.
These women told me often that I was special,
and I finally believed them.

S.N.O.W. Everyday!

Self-Awareness and New Opportunities in Worship

This journal belongs to:

_____

Date

_____

Preface

Are you a person who wants to discover your true uniqueness? Do you want to know how you can see yourself united with others while being in God's presence? **S.N.O.W. Everyday** is just what you need. Don't be surprised if you even grow into a richer relationship with God while you delve into **S.N.O.W. Everyday**.

Snow is necessary for several reasons. God created it, so therefore it has purpose and meaning. Snow purifies and refreshes. Snow paints a beautiful scene. Snow is just plain fun. These are physical aspects of snow. I choose to believe that there is a spiritual side of snow. It is referenced several times in scripture. Just like people, snow has purpose and meaning. It purifies and refreshes, so do people. Just as snow paints a beautiful scene, people are beautiful in their own way. Snow is fun; people like to have fun.

Still there is another aspect of snow. When I think about the billions of tiny ice crystals that come together to make snow, it brings to mind the 6.6 billion people in the world that come together to make contributions in this world one way or another with their uniqueness. Some people use their God-given uniqueness in ways that build up the world. Others unfortunately are busy tearing down the world. Those who are trying to build it up may sometimes feel as if they are so insignificant when they see their place in the world. They may feel that if they are not an Alice

Walker, a Michael W. Smith, an Oprah Winfrey, or a Tyler Perry, who they are and what they do is not important.

S.N.O.W. Everyday seeks to give people a different mindset. It is a guide for reflecting on scripture. It is a journal for expressing your unique thoughts. It is a tool that will help you to see yourself as God created you to be; unique in your own way. As you use **S.N.O.W. Everyday**, it is my desire that you will become more aware of your uniqueness.

S.N.O.W. Everyday!
Reflections of Past Snow

What you are about to read would make a person wonder why would someone like snow when their life began in such a "cold" way! It was a bitter snowy winter day in February, 1956. Funds were not available for Mama to go to a hospital, so I was born in an old farm house which belonged to my maternal grandparents. I am told that being in that house did not necessarily mean that one was kept from the elements outdoors. Old rags were used to keep the wind and snow out from around the windows and doors. Rugs were used to cover the holes in the floors. Mama had been in labor for several hours and at one o'clock, in the afternoon, I finally made the move to depart from the comforts of a warm nourishing womb into the arms of a loving mother. She cared for my siblings and me in spite of the poor living conditions.

Mama was determined to provide whatever she could to make sure her children would grow up and experience a life that was better than the one she had to encounter most of her life. Mama reminded us often that things would not always be difficult, but in order to live a better life, one must work hard, never give up, and trust in God.

For many years, Mama, Daddy, my two older sisters and I lived in a three room house which consisted of a living room, one bedroom and a kitchen. The restroom was an outdoor toilet which sat just outside the kitchen door. After my other sister and two brothers were born, all of us continued to live in that small shelter. My two older sisters and I slept in the living room on a couch that was hardly adequate for one person. One of my brothers slept with Daddy in one bed in the bedroom. My youngest sister and brother slept with Mama in another bed in the same bedroom.

As I write about my early childhood, it seems so unreal. Even with all of the pain and strain that my family had to endure, we were able to get along well. We did not always have the kind of food that we saw on television, but we ate. We did not always have clothes like we saw in the magazines, but we were not naked. We did not have a house that sat on a hill surrounded by green pastures, but we had a place we called home.

During the summer of 1964, I visited my grandparents. Eventually the occasional visit with Grandma and Grandpa turned out to be continuous visits until I was sixteen years old. I often asked Mama why I was chosen to go live with Grandma. She responded by saying that Grandma asked for me to come. When I questioned Grandma, she would tell me that I was special to her.

As my visits in the country continued, I found them to be a time of joy. I began to look forward to June of each year. It was there in the country that I met my best friend. We would sit on the porch and talk for hours as we shelled peas, shucked corn and snapped beans. I would ask the questions, and she always had the answers. It was my best friend who first introduced me to God and the church. Every first and third Sunday we would put on our "Sunday best" and journey off to church. My best friend would tell me often that it was important to got to church. It was there that you could meet God and fellowship with family and friends. Inside the church, hymns were sung with no accompaniment of music. It seemed as if the entire building would shake from the profound preaching and the soul stirring shouting. One day in July, as I was in the midst of the worship experience, I found my way down to the front of the church. To this day, I do not know how I got there. I did not understand what the people were doing as they praised God. All I knew was I wanted to experience the same. On the first Sunday in September of 1966, I moved into a cement pond of cool water and was baptized.

Time went on and when my best friend moved, I moved. She left the country which was in Greenville County, Virginia and relocated to Queens, New York. Just as we had done in the country, my best friend and I would spend a lot of time talking. She would take out her Bible and read to me and explain what she had read. Time continued to move on, and I found myself gaining greater knowledge and faith through the conversations and experiences I had with my best friend, who just happened to be my grandmother.

Grandmother died in the fall of 1988. Somehow as I was sitting in the church at her funeral, I found tears flowing down my face. I was sad because I no longer had my best friend to share all my secrets and concerns. Then suddenly, the sadness turned to joy. My best friend was going to a place of eternal rest. The emptiness I felt turned to fullness. I had memories of her that would be with me forever.

After Grandma's death, it seemed as if I could hear her saying to me, "You are special. You are going to do something special." I could not comprehend why a statement made so many years earlier was so vivid at this stage in my life. By this time, I had spent three years in the United States Army. I had acquired two degrees in education. I began to wonder even more, what was Grandma talking about? I had accomplished so much, but I did not think that they were very special. They were merely moves I made to prepare myself to serve others.

One of my colleagues invited me to a revival. The pastor made an interesting appeal after he had finished preaching. He asked all persons to come forward if they believed God had called them to minister. Several women and men went forward. I was sitting on a pew by myself. I said to myself, "He cannot be talking to me." Suddenly, I heard the pastor make another comment. He thanked the sisters and brothers for being obedient, and then he said, "There is still one more person who has not come forward." I wanted to move and leave the church. I could not move. "Surely, the pastor was not talking to me." That night when I arrived at my house, I fell on my knees beside my bed and wept. Why was I weeping? Why the struggle? What was going on? These questions kept going through my mind daily. I prayed and asked God to show me what this was all about. After several months of communicating with God, I knew without a shadow of a doubt, God was calling me to minister. The times spent with Mama nurturing me, Grandma guiding me, the times spent obtaining degrees in education, the times working in various capacities in the church and the community, and the numerous hours spent studying the Bible, were all part of the preparation for the ministry in which I found myself serving God by serving people.

On the first Sunday in January, 1989, I woke up with a determination to move forward and work in ministry to be a valuable asset to the church and the community. I went to my pastor and told him about what I had been experiencing. He talked and prayed with me. What was so interesting about the conversation was that my pastor said that he was not surprised by what I had told him. After months of training and preparation for ministry, I received my Certificate of License to the Gospel Ministry. It did not dawn on me until years later, that I was the first female to be licensed in the 124 year history of that church. Isn't that special!

In Hebrews, chapter eleven, there is a list of persons who remained faithful to God even in the midst of adversity. Only two women by name are mentioned, Sarah and Rahab. I can easily add three more: my mama, my paternal grandma, and my maternal grandma. These three women really stood the test of time. Mama was determined to raise her six children in a way so that they could contribute positively to society. Grandma Luvenue continued to nurture her grandchildren even when she had already raised nine of her own children. I did not spend a lot of time with Grandma Lucy, but when I did, I remembered she always hit me or anyone else she was near very hard while she made us laugh.

It was these women and countless others, in my life, that taught me much about snow, that is, S.N.O.W. (Self-awareness and New Opportunities in Worship). They taught me to see myself as God created me, that is, a unique human being. They taught me to dream dreams and seek new opportunities to make those dreams become reality. They taught me to spend time worshipping God because it is God who deserved all the praise, honor, and glory for what I do positively with my life.

My life started off with freezing cold snow. A life of "past snow" does not necessarily mean one has to have a lifetime of bitterness and bondage. This life I am living has led me to believe that each individual is unique. Your life can be a joy if you delve into S.N.O.W. Everyday!

Six Weeks?

*"Then God said, "Let us make man in our image, in our likeness, and let them rule over the fish of the sea and the birds of the air, over the livestock, over all the earth, and over all the creatures that move along the ground.
So God created man in his own image,
in the image of God he created him;
male and female he created them.
God saw all that he had made, and it was very good.
And there was evening, and there was morning—
the sixth day."*
Genesis 1:26, 27 and 31

Snow is made from clusters of ice crystals that form from frozen water. Each ice crystal becomes a snowflake that has six sides.

Yes, God created the heavens and the earth in six days. It is scientifically known that the average snowflake has six sides. That's not why this study will take six weeks to complete. Researchers have stated that it takes 15 to 30 days to develop a habit. In that amount of time, you will have developed what the creator of this journal calls a temporary habit. If you want to move beyond the temporary to a permanent lifestyle of seeing and appreciating the real you as you worship daily, then you will make a commitment for six weeks that will change your life beyond your expectations while digging deeper and deeper into **S.N.O.W. Everyday.**

S.N.O.W. Everyday

Week One

Week One: Day 1

*"For you created my inmost being; you knit me together in my mother's womb.
I praise you because I am fearfully and wonderfully made;
your works are wonderful, I know that full well."*
Psalm 139:13-14

Scripture: Read the scripture from three versions of the Bible.

Rewrite the scripture by replacing your name in the text where appropriate.

_____
_____
_____
_____
_____
_____
_____
_____
_____
_____
_____
_____
_____
_____

Week One: Day 2

*"For you created my inmost being; you knit me together in my mother's womb.
I praise you because I am fearfully and wonderfully made;
Your works are wonderful, I know that full well."*
Psalm 139:13-14

Self-Awareness: How does this scripture relate to the unique you?

Name six things that make you unique.

_____
_____
_____
_____
_____
_____
_____
_____
_____
_____
_____
_____
_____
_____

Week One: Day 3

*"For you created my inmost being; you knit me together
in my mother's womb.
I praise you because I am fearfully and
wonderfully made;
your works are wonderful, I know that full well."*
Psalm 139:13-14

Service: How will you minister to the following today?

Myself

My family

My church

My local community

My national community

My world community

Week One: Day 4

*"For you created my inmost being; you knit me together in my mother's womb.
I praise you because I am fearfully and wonderfully made;
your works are wonderful, I know that full well."*
Psalm 139:13-14

Source of Strength:

Who is the one person you can depend on today to help the unique you?

Name six ways he or she can help you.

_____
_____
_____
_____
_____
_____
_____
_____
_____
_____
_____
_____
_____

Week One: Day 5

*"For you created my inmost being; you knit me together in my mother's womb.
I praise you because I am fearfully and wonderfully made;
your works are wonderful, I know that full well."*
Psalm 139:13-14

Song: What song/hymn inspires the unique you today?

Listen to the song/hymn.

Name six ways the song/hymn inspires you.

_____
_____
_____
_____
_____
_____
_____
_____
_____
_____
_____
_____
_____

Week One: Day 6

*"For you created my inmost being; you knit me together in my mother's womb.
I praise you because I am fearfully and wonderfully made;
Your works are wonderful, I know that full well."*
Psalm 139:13-14

Simple Prayer: Write a prayer thanking God for the unique you.

_____
_____
_____
_____
_____
_____
_____
_____
_____
_____
_____
_____
_____
_____
_____
_____

Week One: Day 7

*"For you created my inmost being; you knit me together in my mother's womb.
I praise you because I am fearfully and wonderfully made;
your works are wonderful, I know that full well."*
Psalm 139:13-14

Summary: What new opportunities did you discover this week while in God's presence?

_____
_____
_____
_____
_____
_____
_____
_____
_____
_____
_____
_____
_____
_____
_____
_____

S.N.O.W. Everyday

Week Two

Week Two: Day 1

*"Come now, let us reason together," says the LORD.
Though your sins are like scarlet, they shall be
as white as snow;
though they are red as crimson, they shall be like wool."*
Isaiah 1:18

Scripture: Read the scripture from three versions of the Bible.

Rewrite the scripture by replacing your name in the text where appropriate.

_____
_____
_____
_____
_____
_____
_____
_____
_____
_____
_____
_____
_____
_____
_____
_____

Week Two: Day 2

*"Come now, let us reason together," says the LORD.
"Though your sins are like scarlet, they shall be
as white as snow;
though they are red as crimson, they shall be like wool."*
Isaiah 1:18

Self-Awareness: How does this scripture relate to the unique you?

Name six things that make you unique.

_____
_____
_____
_____
_____
_____
_____
_____
_____
_____
_____
_____
_____
_____
_____
_____

Week Two: Day 3

*"Come now, let us reason together," says the LORD.
"Though your sins are like scarlet, they shall be
as white as snow;
though they are red as crimson, they shall be like wool."*
Isaiah 1:18

Service: How will you minister to the following today?

Myself

My family

My church

My local community

My national community

My world community

Week Two: Day 4

"Come now, let us reason together," says the LORD.
"Though your sins are like scarlet, they shall be
as white as snow;
"Though they are red as crimson, they shall be like wool."
Isaiah 1:18

Source of Strength:

Who is the one person you can depend on today to help the unique you?

Name six ways he or she can help you.

Week Two: Day 5

*"Come now, let us reason together," says the LORD.
"Though your sins are like scarlet, they shall be
as white as snow;
though they are red as crimson, they shall be like wool."*
Isaiah 1:18

Song: What song/hymn inspires the unique you today?

Listen to the song/hymn.

Name six ways the song/hymn inspires you.

_____
_____
_____
_____
_____
_____
_____
_____
_____
_____
_____
_____
_____
_____

Week Two: Day 6

"Come now, let us reason together," says the LORD. "Though your sins are like scarlet, they shall be as white as snow; though they are red as crimson, they shall be like wool."
Isaiah 1:18

Simple Prayer: Write a prayer thanking God for the unique you.

Week Two: Day 7

*"Come now, let us reason together," says the LORD.
"Though your sins are like scarlet, they shall be
as white as snow;
though they are red as crimson, they shall be like wool."*
Isaiah 1:18

Summary: What new opportunities did you discover this week while in God's presence?

_____

_____

_____

_____

_____

_____

_____

_____

_____

_____

_____

_____

_____

_____

_____

_____

S.N.O.W. Everyday

Week Three

Week Three: Day 1

"Cleanse me with hyssop, and I will be clean;
"Wash me, and I will be whiter than snow."
Psalm 51:7

Scripture: Read the scripture from three versions of the Bible.

Rewrite the scripture by replacing your name in the text where appropriate.

Week Three: Day 2

"Cleanse me with hyssop, and I will be clean; wash me, and I will be whiter than snow."
Psalm 51:7

Self-Awareness: How does this scripture relate to the unique you?

Name six things that make you unique.

Week Three: Day 3

*"Cleanse me with hyssop, and I will be clean;
wash me, and I will be whiter than snow."*
Psalm 51:7

Service: How will you minister to the following today?

Myself

My family

My church

My local community

My national community

My world community

Week Three: Day 4

"Cleanse me with hyssop, and I will be clean; wash me, and I will be whiter than snow."
Psalm 51:7

Sources of Strength:

Who is the one person you can depend on today to help the unique you?

Name six ways he or she can help you.

Week Three: Day 5

"Cleanse me with hyssop, and I will be clean; wash me, and I will be whiter than snow."
Psalm 51:7

Song: What song/hymn inspires the unique you today?

Listen to the song/hymn.

Name six ways the song/hymn inspires you.

_____
_____
_____
_____
_____
_____
_____
_____
_____
_____
_____
_____
_____
_____
_____
_____
_____

Week Three: Day 6

"Cleanse me with hyssop, and I will be clean; wash me, and I will be whiter than snow."
Psalm 51:7

Simple Prayer: Write a prayer thanking God for the unique you.

Week Three: Day 7

"Cleanse me with hyssop, and I will be clean; wash me, and I will be whiter than snow."
Psalm 51:7

Summary: What new opportunities did you discover this week while in God's presence?

S.N.O.W. Everyday

Week Four

Week Four: Day 1

*"God's voice thunders in marvelous ways;
he does great things beyond our understanding.
He says to the snow, 'Fall on the earth,'
and to the rain shower, 'Be a mighty downpour'."*
Job 37:5-6

Scripture: Read the scripture from three versions of the Bible.

Rewrite the scripture by replacing your name in the text where appropriate.

Week Four: Day 2

*"God's voice thunders in marvelous ways;
he does great things beyond our understanding.
He says to the snow, 'Fall on the earth,'
and to the rain shower, 'Be a mighty downpour'."*
Job 37:5-6

Self-Awareness: How does this scripture relate to the unique you?

Name six things that make you unique.

Week Four: Day 3

*"God's voice thunders in marvelous ways;
he does great things beyond our understanding.
He says to the snow, 'Fall on the earth,'
and to the rain shower, 'Be a mighty downpour'."*
Job 37:5-6

Service: How will you minister to the following today?

Myself

My family

My church

My local community

My national community

My world community

S.N.O.W. Everyday!

Week Four: Day 4

*"God's voice thunders in marvelous ways;
he does great things beyond our understanding.
He says to the snow, 'Fall on the earth,'
and to the rain shower, 'Be a mighty downpour'."*
Job 37:5-6

Sources of Strength:

Who is the one person you can depend on today to help the unique you?

Name six ways he or she can help you.

Week Four: Day 5

"God's voice thunders in marvelous ways;
he does great things beyond our understanding.
He says to the snow, 'Fall on the earth,'
and to the rain shower, 'Be a mighty downpour'."
Job 37:5-6

Song: What song/hymn inspires the unique you today?

Listen to the song/hymn.

Name six ways the song/hymn inspires you.

Week Four: Day 6

*"God's voice thunders in marvelous ways;
he does great things beyond our understanding.
He says to the snow, 'Fall on the earth,'
and to the rain shower, 'Be a mighty downpour'."*
Job 37:5-6

Simple Prayer: Write a prayer thanking God for the unique you.

_____
_____
_____
_____
_____
_____
_____
_____
_____
_____
_____
_____
_____
_____
_____
_____
_____
_____
_____
_____

Week Four: Day 7

*"God's voice thunders in marvelous ways;
he does great things beyond our understanding.
He says to the snow, 'Fall on the earth,'
and to the rain shower, 'Be a mighty downpour'."*
Job 37:5-6

Summary: What new opportunities did you discover this week while in God's presence?

_____
_____
_____
_____
_____
_____
_____
_____
_____
_____
_____
_____
_____
_____
_____
_____
_____

S.N.O.W. Everyday

Week Five

Week Five: Day 1

"A wife of noble character who can find?
She is worth far more than rubies.
When it snows, she has no fear for her household;
for all of them are clothed in scarlet."
Proverbs 31:10,21

Scripture: Read the scripture from three versions of the Bible.

Rewrite the scripture by replacing your name in the scripture where appropriate.

Week Five: Day 2

*"A wife of noble character who can find?
She is worth far more than rubies.
When it snows, she has no fear for her household;
for all of them are clothed in scarlet."*
Proverbs 31:10,21

Self-Awareness: How does this scripture relate to the unique you?

Name six things that make you unique.

_____
_____
_____
_____
_____
_____
_____
_____
_____
_____
_____
_____
_____
_____
_____
_____

Week Five: Day 3

*"A wife of noble character who can find?
She is worth far more than rubies.
When it snows, she has no fear for her household;
for all of them are clothed in scarlet."*
Proverbs 31:10,21

Service: How will you minister to the following today?

Myself

My family

My church

My local community

My national community

My world community

S.N.O.W. Everyday!

Week Five: Day 4

*"A wife of noble character who can find?
She is worth far more than rubies.
When it snows, she has no fear for her household;
for all of them are clothed in scarlet."*
Proverbs 31:10,21

Source of Strength:

Who is the one person you can depend on today to help the unique you?

Name six ways he or she can help you.

Week Five: Day 5

"A wife of noble character who can find?
She is worth far more than rubies.
When it snows, she has no fear for her household;
for all of them are clothed in scarlet."
Proverbs 31:10,21

Song: What song/hymn inspires the unique you today?

Listen to the song/hymn.

Name six ways the song/hymn inspires you.

_____
_____
_____
_____
_____
_____
_____
_____
_____
_____
_____
_____
_____
_____

Week Five: Day 6

"A wife of noble character who can find?
She is worth far more than rubies.
When it snows, she has no fear for her household;
for all of them are clothed in scarlet."
Proverbs 31:10,21

Simple Prayer: Write a prayer thanking God for the unique you.

Week Five: Day 7

*"A wife of noble character who can find?
She is worth far more than rubies.
When it snows, she has no fear for her household;
for all of them are clothed in scarlet."*
Proverbs 31:10,21

Summary: What new opportunities did you discover this week while in God's presence?

_____
_____
_____
_____
_____
_____
_____
_____
_____
_____
_____
_____
_____
_____
_____
_____

S.N.O.W. Everyday

Week Six

Week Six: Day 1

*"Now after six days Jesus took Peter, James, and John, and led them up on a high mountain apart by themselves; and He was transfigured before them.
His clothes became shining, exceedingly white, like snow, such as no launderer on earth can whiten them."*
Mark 9:2-3 (New King James Version)

Scripture: Read the scripture from three versions of the Bible.

Rewrite the scripture by replacing your name in the text where appropriate.

_____
_____
_____
_____
_____
_____
_____
_____
_____
_____
_____
_____
_____
_____

Week Six: Day 2

"Now after six days Jesus took Peter, James, and John, and led them up on a high mountain apart by themselves; and He was transfigured before them.
His clothes became shining, exceedingly white, like snow, such as no launderer on earth can whiten them."
Mark 9:2-3 (New King James Version)

Self-Awareness: How does this scripture relate to the unique you?

Name six things that make you unique.

Week Six: Day 3

*"Now after six days Jesus took Peter, James, and John, and led them up on a high mountain apart by themselves; and He was transfigured before them.
His clothes became shining, exceedingly white, like snow, such as no launderer on earth can whiten them."*
Mark 9:2-3 (New King James Version)

Service: How will you minister to the following today?

Myself

My family

My church

My local community

My national community

My world community

Week Six: Day 4

*"Now after six days Jesus took Peter, James, and John, and led them up on a high mountain apart by themselves; and He was transfigured before them.
His clothes became shining, exceedingly white, like snow, such as no launderer on earth can whiten them."*
Mark 9:2-3 (New King James Version)

Source of Strength:

Who is the one person you can depend on today to help the unique you?

Name six ways he or she can help you.

Week Six: Day 5

*"Now after six days Jesus took Peter, James, and John, and led them up on a high mountain apart by themselves; and He was transfigured before them.
His clothes became shining, exceedingly white, like snow, such as no launderer on earth can whiten them."*
Mark 9:2-3 (New King James Version)

Song: What song/hymn inspires the unique you today?

Listen to the song/hymn.

Name six ways the song/hymn inspires you.

_____
_____
_____
_____
_____
_____
_____
_____
_____
_____
_____
_____

Week Six: Day 6

"Now after six days Jesus took Peter, James, and John, and led them up on a high mountain apart by themselves; and He was transfigured before them. His clothes became shining, exceedingly white, like snow, such as no launderer on earth can whiten them."
Mark 9:2-3 (New King James Version)

Simple Prayer: Write a prayer thanking God for the unique you.

_____
_____
_____
_____
_____
_____
_____
_____
_____
_____
_____
_____
_____
_____

Week Six: Day 7

"Now after six days Jesus took Peter, James, and John, and led them up on a high mountain apart by themselves; and He was transfigured before them.
His clothes became shining, exceedingly white, like snow, such as no launderer on earth can whiten them."
Mark 9:2-3 (New King James Version)

Summary: What new opportunities did you discover this week while in God's presence?

_____
_____
_____
_____
_____
_____
_____
_____
_____
_____
_____
_____
_____
_____
_____
_____

S.N.O.W. Everyday!
"A Choice"

You have been there. At one time or another, you did not think of yourself in the best way. You may have referred to yourself as too short, too tall, too skinny, too fat, too dark, too light, too dumb, too clumsy, too, too, too, and the list goes on. You are a created being of God. When God first formed you in your mother's womb, God knew what you were going to look like. It has been up to you as to what you have done and will do with the precious gift of life you have received. It is up to you to listen to the words of God as you have reflected in this journal to guide you in living a life of being special to yourself and in the presence of God and others. From this time on, stop listening to the voices of negative thoughts and words. Start celebrating the unique you and thank God for the life that you have been given.

Snow can be viewed in at least two ways; bad snow and good snow. Bad snow freezes and makes it difficult to drive or walk. Bad snow destroys crops and other things in nature. On the other hand, good snow insulates and blankets nature with beauty. Doesn't it feel good to have experienced some "good" snow for these past six weeks? Doesn't it feel good that for these past six weeks you have focused on the unique you and not all the bad or negative things about you? Aren't you glad you took the time to change or enhance your view of you? Don't stop now!

Start this process all over again for the rest of this year or even for the rest of your life. You will experience daily that you are "fearfully and wonderfully made" while you keep delving into S.N.O.W. Everyday.

S.N.O.W. Everyday!

Bonus Bible Study

Self-Awareness of the Unique You

Read the statements below:
Remember a time when each one of the statements made you feel unique.

- You were created by God.
- You have at least one spiritual gift.
- You felt good about doing something for someone.
- You accepted a compliment.
- You ignored a negative comment.
- You praised God when you were in the midst of a situation or challenge.

New Insights from Psalm 8:1-9

Read Psalm 8
Underline the best answer for each statement.
Psalm 8:1
   In worship, we mainly look (downward, upward) toward God.
   In worship, God's name is (ultimately, never) to be praised.
Psalm 8:2
   Even (chairs, children) can praise God.

Enemies are silenced when believers (curse, celebrate) God.

Psalm 8:3

People are overwhelmed when thinking about the (pain, plan) of God's creation.
God (placed, threw) the heavens, the moon and stars in space.

Psalm 8:4-5

God (created, crushed) humans and cares for them.
God (crowned, ignores) humans with glory and honor

Psalm 8:6-9

Everything is (up in the air, under the feet) of humans.
The (unique, dangerous) place of humans comes from God.

Opportunities for Practical Application

Think of six ways you can apply Psalm 8 in your life.

Worship through inspirational hymns

Read the lyrics or listen to the following hymns:
"How Great Thou Art"
"His Eye Is On the Sparrow"
How do these hymns help you see the unique you?

Spend time in prayer and thank God for the unique you.

CPSIA information can be obtained at www.ICGtesting.com
263034BV00001B/2/P